Spotlight on
Kids Can Code

What Is
GEOLOCATION?

Patricia Harris

PowerKiDS press
New York

Published in 2018 by The Rosen Publishing Group, Inc.
29 East 21st Street, New York, NY 10010

Copyright © 2018 by The Rosen Publishing Group, Inc.

All rights reserved. No part of this book may be reproduced in any form without permission in writing from the publisher, except by a reviewer.

First Edition

Editor: Melissa Raé Shofner
Book Design: Michael J. Flynn

Photo Credits: Cover (main) FamVeld/Shutterstock.com; cover (map) A7880S/Shutterstock.com; pp. 1, 3-24 (background) Lukas Rs/Shutterstock.com; p. 5 Andrey_Popov/Shutterstock.com; p. 7 Rafal Olechowski/Shutterstock.com; p. 9 Lithiumphoto/Shutterstock.com; p. 11 (top) HKPNC/E+/Getty Images; p. 11 (bottom) Lasse Hendriks/Shutterstock.com; p. 13 KeongDaGreat/Shutterstock.com; p. 15 Arina P Habich/Shutterstock.com; p. 17 Dean Mitchell/E+/Getty Images; p. 19 Don Johnston/All Canada Photos/Getty Images; p. 21 (top) ekkasit919/Shutterstock.com; p. 21 (bottom) dennizn/Shutterstock.com.

Cataloging-in-Publication Data

Names: Harris, Patricia.
Title: What is geolocation? / Patricia Harris.
Description: New York : PowerKids Press, 2018. | Series: Spotlight on kids can code | Includes index.
Identifiers: ISBN 9781508155294 (pbk.) | ISBN 9781508155188 (library bound) | ISBN 9781508154839 (6 pack)
Subjects: LCSH: Mobile geographic information systems. | Mobile communication systems. | Global Positioning System.
Classification: LCC G70.212 H37 2018 | DDC 910.285–dc23

Manufactured in the United States of America

CPSIA Compliance Information: Batch #BS17PK: For Further Information contact Rosen Publishing, New York, New York at 1-800-237-9932

Contents

Finding the Location.....................4
Geolocation Systems....................6
The History of GPS.....................8
Geocaching............................10
Pokémon GO..........................12
Geofencing............................14
Tracking Animals with GPS.............18
Advertising with Beacons..............20
Staying Safe..........................22
Glossary..............................23
Index.................................24
Websites..............................24

Finding the Location

Geolocation is a process by which people can figure out the location of something, such as a computer or a mobile device, using information sent over the Internet. Geolocation may also refer to a location itself.

What does this all mean? It means you can use a map **application (app)** on your phone to give you directions to a new place from your current location. It means your family's car can use a service that, when activated in an emergency, will know where the car is located and send help. It means scientists can track animals to better understand their movements in the wild. It means your parents can know where you are when you're out with friends. It means that you and thousands of other people can play location-based games such as *Pokémon GO* together.

Geolocation lets your computer or smartphone identify where it is. It can also let others know your location.

Geolocation Systems

When people think of geolocation, they often think of the global positioning system, or GPS. GPS is a **satellite** system that provides location data to GPS receivers. This data can be used to figure out the position and speed of vehicles and other devices with receivers. To work, a receiver must be able to connect to at least three satellites. The system isn't affected by weather and it doesn't need Internet or phone service to work.

Some geolocation systems measure the time a cell phone signal takes to reach a cellular **network** tower and use this information to figure out location. They do this by looking at the distances between the signal and three towers. This is called triangulation. An **Internet Protocol (IP) address** may also be used to determine general location. Any device that uses the Internet has an IP address.

GPS was first used in cars in the 1990s. Today, people can use GPS to get directions while driving, to locate their car if it's stolen, and even to lock the doors and roll up the windows when they're not there!

The History of GPS

GPS started as a military system developed by the U.S. Department of Defense. It was created in response to the **Cold War**. In 1983, the Soviet Union shot down an aircraft that strayed into Soviet airspace. This prompted President Ronald Reagan to grant access to GPS for commercial aircraft. A "selective access" policy gave the public a lower level of access than members of the military. In 2000, President Bill Clinton gave the same level of GPS access to everyone.

GPS may seem confusing, but it's actually quite simple. The system has three main segments, or parts. The control segment is made up of stations on Earth that send data to and receive it from satellites. The satellites make up the space segment. They orbit Earth and send signals to the stations and devices. The individual users and their GPS-enabled devices make up the user segment.

Without interference, your smartphone's GPS may be able to tell your location within about 16 feet (4.9 m). The most powerful military GPS units are much more exact.

Breaking the Code

Smartphones may use what is called assisted GPS. When a smartphone is within a cellular network area, assisted GPS may be able to use cell tower triangulation to boost the GPS information being sent from satellites. This allows users to access GPS data faster while using less battery life and processing power.

Geocaching

Geocaching, first described in early 2000, is a game that uses GPS **coordinates** to lead players to hidden containers in the real world. In geocaching, these containers are called "caches." Caches may be large buckets, tiny boxes, or anything in between. They often contain a notebook for signing in when you find the cache and small items for trading. Players find coordinates for a cache from a website or app, then use a GPS device to find the location.

A number of games have been developed around geocaching. Some have special rules and time limits in which to find a location. One game, called geodashing, requires players to either be the first to a location or to find the most locations within a set amount of time. There are millions of geocache locations around the world.

Players may take an item from a cache as long as they put something of equal or greater value back into the container.

GEOCACHE, DO NOT REMOVE

11

Pokémon GO

Pokémon GO is a popular location-based augmented reality game. In this game, players use their smartphone's GPS to locate **virtual** creatures called Pokémon in real-world locations. As players move around in real life, their character moves on the in-game map. Different creatures appear in different places. For example, water-type Pokémon appear when a player walks near a lake.

While playing the game, a player can use their smartphone's camera to view the in-game creatures in real-world settings on their screen. When a player finds a Pokémon, they can tap the camera symbol in the game to switch from a virtual view to a view of what the camera sees in the real world. If a player is standing in their backyard when they find a Pokémon, they'll be able to "see" the virtual creature standing in their real-life backyard on their screen!

Millions of people around the world play *Pokémon GO* on their smartphones every day. It's been very popular since it was launched in 2016.

Breaking the Code

Pokémon GO is important because it's introduced millions of people to what is known as augmented reality (AR) programming. AR is computer **software** that combines a view of the real world with sound, video, or images created by a computer.

Geofencing

A geofence is a virtual boundary, or fence, around a real-life area. GPS is sometimes used to define, or set, these boundaries. When a mobile device enters or leaves an area surrounded by a geofence, it sets off special software. This software may send alerts to the mobile device or cause the device to perform other actions.

When geofencing was first created, it wasn't available to many people. It had very specific uses and was expensive because special **hardware** was needed. Today, smartphones come with this hardware built in. Computer application developers can design software that is able to interface with a geofence.

Geofencing is being used more and more as we ask our smartphones and other devices within the **Internet of things** to do more for us. Geofencing allows us to be automatically reminded and alerted of things when we cross virtual boundaries.

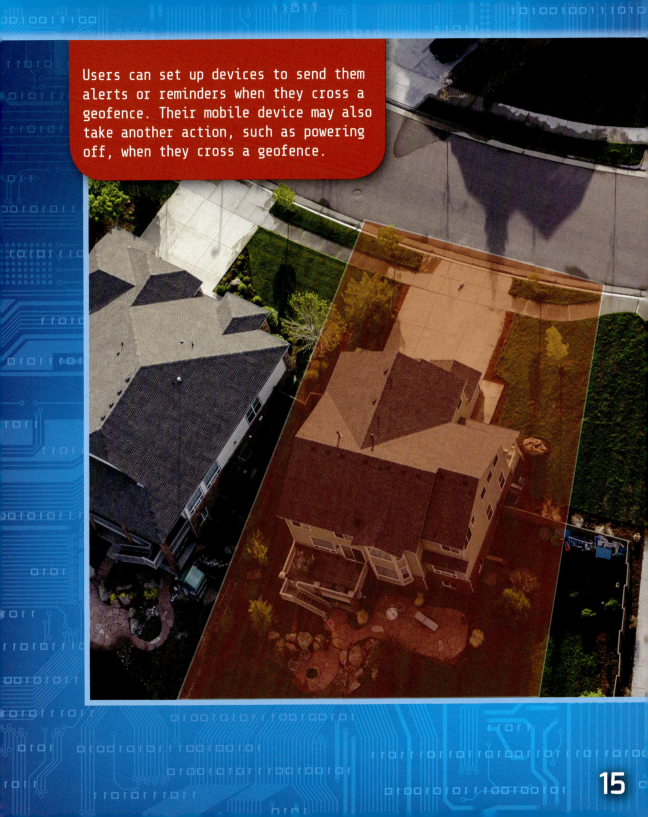

Users can set up devices to send them alerts or reminders when they cross a geofence. Their mobile device may also take another action, such as powering off, when they cross a geofence.

Geofencing has many uses. There are apps that can remind a user to do something when they're near a specific location.

Smart home control is another use of geofencing. Some mobile apps can turn on a user's house lights as they approach their home. Users can also connect to their home's heating system so their furnace turns on when they cross a geofence set up around their house.

A third use allows users to keep track of the location of other people or objects. For example, parents can buy simple wristbands, or bracelets, that use GPS to track their child's location. Parents may also set up a geofence and receive alerts if their child crosses the boundary. Similar devices are available for elderly people who have memory problems. The devices can alert caregivers if a person leaves a certain area.

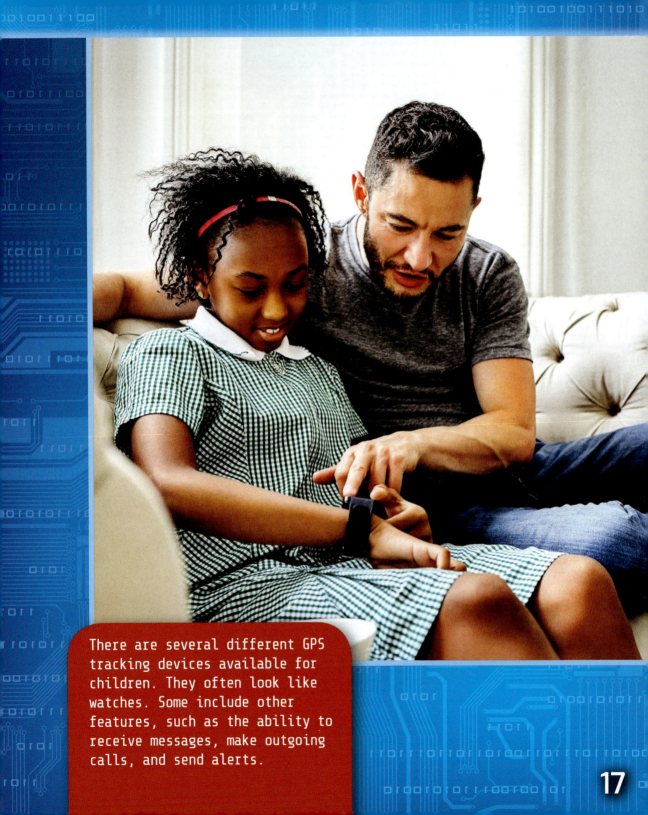

There are several different GPS tracking devices available for children. They often look like watches. Some include other features, such as the ability to receive messages, make outgoing calls, and send alerts.

17

Tracking Animals with GPS

Some people use geolocation to track their pets. Special GPS-enabled collars let people see where their pets have gone. Users may even create a geofence around their yard or another area and receive an alert if their pet crosses the boundary.

Scientists use geolocation to study how animals in the wild move, often in relation to **climate change** and **habitat** loss. They're able to track all sorts of animals, even birds and creatures that live underwater, using special GPS devices. Larger animals, such as bears and wolves, may be fitted with GPS-enabled collars. Small GPS devices have been stuck to turtles using waterproof glue.

Sometimes GPS data from a device is sent directly to special receivers. It may even be sent directly to an app on a scientist's smartphone! Other times, the data is retrieved when a GPS-enabled device is removed from an animal.

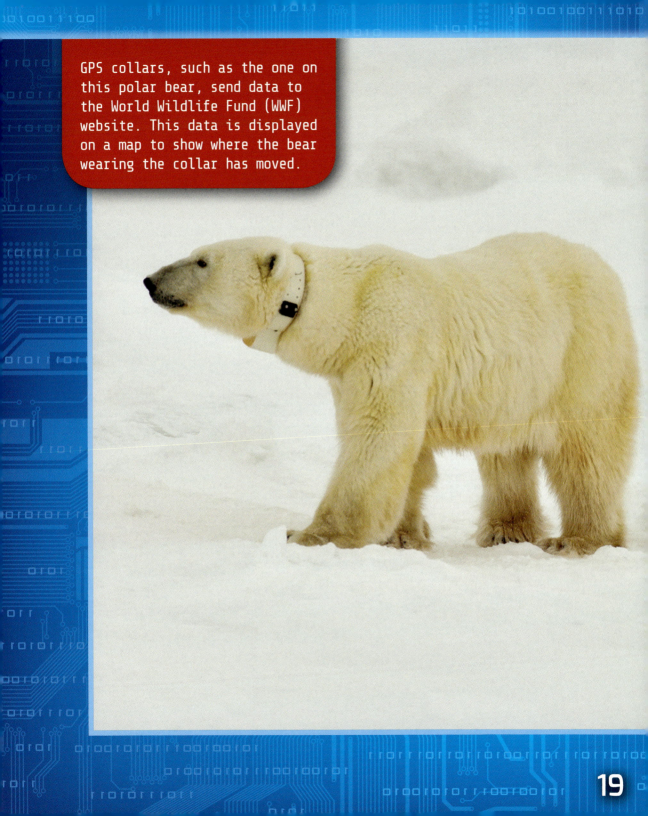

GPS collars, such as the one on this polar bear, send data to the World Wildlife Fund (WWF) website. This data is displayed on a map to show where the bear wearing the collar has moved.

Advertising with Beacons

A fairly new development using geolocation is the use of beacons in advertising. Beacons are small devices that send out low-energy signals. They're battery powered, can fit in many places, and work with mobile apps. If a store uses beacons, customers may be sent special messages while they're in or near that store. They may receive advertisements to try to get them to buy more things.

To receive these message and ads, customers need to have a special app on their phone that "listens" for beacon signals. When the smartphone user enters the range of a beacon, the app picks up the signal and sends the beacon's ID to the phone. Then the phone sends the ID to the **cloud**. The cloud interprets the ID and sends a message or advertisement back to the phone.

Users with a beacon app who walk in or near a store may receive messages such as "All produce 15% off today only!" or "Sale! Fresh bread. Buy one, get one free!"

21

Staying Safe

Geolocation is proving to be a valuable tool for the military, governments, businesses, and even gamers! However, access to geolocation services brings up several concerns.

One issue with geolocation is the use of the devices with children. At what age, if any, is the use of tracking devices wrong? Adults have a right to privacy, but those rights are unclear for people under 18. The laws seem to suggest that parents can legally track their children. Children and their parents should talk about when the tracking features can or should be turned off.

Geolocation gives social media users the ability to "check in" to their location online. It's easier than ever to let your friends and family know where you are through social networking sites. Strangers may also be able to see your location, though. Always use caution when sharing your location online.

Glossary

application (app): A program that performs one of the tasks for which a computer, smartphone, or tablet is used.

climate change: Change in Earth's weather caused by human activity.

cloud: A large network of servers where data may be stored, accessed, and shared.

Cold War: The nonviolent conflict between the United States and the Soviet Union during the second half of the 20th century.

coordinates: A set of numbers used to indicate the location of a point on a line, in space, or on a surface.

habitat: The natural home for plants, animals, and other living things.

hardware: The physical parts of a computer system, such as wires, hard drives, keyboards, and monitors.

Internet of things: The network of household devices and other items that can send and receive data through the Internet.

Internet protocol (IP) address: The numeric address of a computer on the Internet.

network: A system of computers and databases that are all connected.

satellite: A spacecraft placed in orbit around Earth, a moon, or a planet to collect information or to be used for communication.

software: A program that runs on a computer and performs certain tasks.

virtual: Occurring or existing primarily on a computer or online.

Index

A
animals, 4, 18
application (app), 4, 10, 14, 16, 18, 20, 21
assisted GPS, 9
augmented reality (AR), 12, 13

B
beacons, 20, 21

C
cellular network, 6, 9
Clinton, Bill, 8
cloud, 20
Cold War, 8

D
Defense, U.S. Department of, 8

G
geocaching, 10, 11
geodashing, 10
geofence, 14, 15, 16, 18
global positioning system (GPS), 6, 7, 8, 9, 10, 12, 14, 16, 17, 18, 19

H
hardware, 14

I
Internet of things, 14
Internet Protocol (IP) address, 6

M
military, 8, 9, 22

P
Pokémon Go, 4, 12, 13

R
Reagan, Ronald, 8
receivers, 6, 18

S
satellites, 6, 8, 9
software, 13, 14
Soviet Union, 8

T
triangulation, 6, 9

W
World Wildlife Fund, 19

Websites

Due to the changing nature of Internet links, PowerKids Press has developed an online list of websites related to the subject of this book. This site is updated regularly. Please use this link to access the list: www.powerkidslinks.com/skcc/geo